2001: a space ode and ditty
by
Colin J Davies

Cover Design and Illustrations by **Colin Davies**
Proof Reader - **Moyra Davies**
Edited by **Ashley R Lister**

Published by Word Rabbit Books via Lulu 2015

ISBN 978-1-326-40185-6

TOP MENU (INDEX)

MAIN FEATURE .. p13

SPECIAL FEATURES

DVD Extra - The Making of '2001: a space ode and ditty'

I had been thinking about writing a show about my love of all things geek for a while. My original idea was to just write a collection of poems all based on sci-fi, horror and fantasy. Then in June 2014 I did something that changed that plan.

My partner was taking our son on a little trip away during his October half-term. Being as I wasn't going with them I thought I'd plan a little trip of my own to visit some friends in the south of England. I had decided to stop with my friend Matt in Greenwich, with a trip to see, and hopefully perform, an open mic slot at 'Bang Said the Gun' at Great Dover Street, London.

From there I would travel to my old home town of Brighton, spend the weekend with my oldest friend Dylan and then travel back home in time for the return of my family. So everything was being organised for the Halloween weekend. I checked the internet to see if there was anything special happening on the south coast I could go to.

The searches revealed a brand new convention called WynterCon in Eastbourne. Now I hadn't been to a convention for a few years, well since my son came along, so this seemed like a perfect fit. It was then the idea hit me: what if I could perform a poetry show at this convention?

Now I do know a couple of spoken word shows involving fandom have been doing the rounds, Rod Tame has some great Doctor Who stuff and Mark Grist touched on the subject on his *Rogue Teacher* tour. But I was unaware of anyone doing an entire show, and what's more, I had not heard of anyone doing a spoken word show at a ComicCon before.

I fired off an email to the organiser, Andy Kybett, claiming to already be working on a show: a sort of hit and hope. Ten minutes after the email was sent Andy phoned me, we discussed the idea and next thing I know I was booked to perform at WynterCon. I was ecstatic; all I had to do then was write the thing.

Once I had chosen which stories to tell; written all the poetry to complement them; ordered them; decided that they didn't work and rewritten them four times; panicked because I was running out of time; operated on three hours sleep a night through August and September and finally had something I was happy with, it was time to try it out on an audience.

With two weeks to go before WynterCon I booked a venue in Blackpool and in front of a specially invited audience, performed *2001: a space ode and ditty* for the first time. That warm up show was so valuable to tightening to whole show. With the feedback and my own observations, I was able to fine tune the show and deliver a much more complete and professional piece.

At midday on the 1st of November 2014 I took to the stage for the first time in front of an audience where I didn't know the majority of the people and was delighted with how it was received. A second show followed day after. These two performances, plus the one in Blackpool, qualified it for the Saboteur Awards as show of the year. It got enough nominations to be shortlisted and enough votes to be the 3rd best spoken word show in the UK 2015.

An extended version of the show *2001: a space ode and ditty (the director's cut)* is being developed with video presentations, on stage and sound effects. I am hoping to have this ready for mid 2016.

The book you are about to read is the show I wrote. OK it's not the actual as it's had a slight polish with some additions to make it more of a reading experience than the show however, what is published here is 90% of the script performed.

There is one new poem written after the shows went out (Drawn is the Story), and all the poems including the ones cut from some of the performance (My Forty Second Character was cut from the final show) are all here.

A couple of the poems have been published before. Both *Good Bye Dad* and *My Kingdom* feature in *The Book Of Colin: a complete (at time of going to press) collection of poetry (c.2014)*.

The poem *What Future?* also appeared in *The Book Of Colin* only here the end has been re-written so that it connects better with the story.

There are two found poems in this book and even though I have identified the texts and ordered them into a poetic form, please read the notes found at the end to see who actually wrote the words.

Some of the names in these stories have been changed and some haven't. In order to keep it fair I will not mention which is which. Those who know will understand while those that don't will be none the wiser.

I hope you enjoy these stories as much as I enjoyed living them.

DVD Extra - Foreword by Sean Payne

Writing a love song should be easy. We have all done it, fallen in love, had our hearts broken, battled on and come through with scars and wisdom, so writing that love song should be easy, but it's not, it's the hardest thing in the world.

For every heart-breaking/affirming classic, you can find a thousand 'girl I dig you' boy band songs cluttering the airwaves. The great love song has a touch of the universal, one toe in the collective unconscious that transforms the words into a testament to the very nature of loving that boy/girl. To walk that tightrope between schmaltz and sincerity is a perilous thing, the great love songs find that balance and we hold them to our hearts because we recognise the truths within them.

You hold in your hand a great love song. What Davies has achieved here in these pages is that testament to his time and love to what is now termed 'Geek-Life', predating the current trend of superhero movies and hipster chic, what I like to call 'Pre-BBT' (Big Bang Theory) when being a geek was something you tended to keep secret, like those Warhammer figures you hid whenever someone came round to the house.

His lines paint us a personal journey through the myriad of geek pathways, much like the character sheet of a role-playing game, this book gives us the stats and the skills of Colin Davies star traveller and tells us of an epic adventure through the worlds of Dr Who, Blake's 7, Judge Dredd and 1980s horror films. It is a flawless series of snapshots that paint a life lived and enriched by having those other selves, the one that travels in the TARDIS, shoots perps with our Lawgivers and has an unhealthy crush on Avon from Blake's 7.

After seeing the warm up show in 2014 I was quite excited about reading this book, and even though he has still forgotten to include a poem about the best film ever made Hawk the Slayer, (1980) I can forgive him. Davies manages to be universal yet personal, funny yet poignant and creates something which speaks to all of us who ended up in a strange love affair with the odd worlds of telefantasy, films and comics. You will enjoy it, you will laugh, you will be moved, you will be assimilated.

Sean Payne is a Blackpool based artist and writer who spends far too long in the back garden looking for the mothership to take him home.

DVD Extra: A big thank you.

I have so many people to thank. As always I have to say a massive thank you to my partner Heather Brennan. She has to put up with me when I'm in writing mode, and with this project she's had to live through it twice so far, so I think it's only fair she gets double thanks.

My mum gets a massive thank you. It's always worth remembering that without your parents you can't write memoirs. Sticking with family I also have to thank my brother Ray. His input was fantastic and really helped shape the final piece.

Special mentions of thanks go out to my very good friends Simon Hart; Louise Barklam; Joy France; Sean Payne; Debbie Wood; Steve Stroud; Mick Arthur and George Stephenson for all you fantastic feedback after the warm up. I also have to thank Jason Brashill for his wonderful suggestions during the writing process.

More thanks to Matthew Bartlett; Dylan Freeman; Jock & Prency O'Connor; The Wright family; Tony & Jonathon McMullan and Iayn Dobsyn for coming along to WynterCon to support me as well as helping me write the history that I have drawn from to create this work.

Working with talented people always makes it easier to achieve your goals. Many thanks go to Ashley R Lister, not only for being a fantastic editor but also for being a really good friend.

More thanks than I know how to give goes to Andy Kybett. It was his faith in concept and in me that really made all this possible. He and the WynterCon team had a big dream for an all genre convention, and I am so proud to have been part of their journey as they have been a massive part of mine.

The last of my gratitude's has to go to all the creatives, writers, actors, artists, directors, coders, publishers and studios that have delivered all the books, films, TV programmes, games and toys that have filled my life with such wonder. It is their visions and ideas that fuelled, and keep on fuelling the imaginations of children and adults all around the world. The big businesses at the top might be all about the ching of the cash register but, nevertheless, those that create the monsters and heroes and worlds; the artifacts and books and spells; those who dare to see a world beyond our time where the Judges are the law and a lost mining ships carries the last of the human race: I salute you all.

"We are the music makers, and
we are the dreamers of dreams."
(Willy Wonka: Willy Wonka and the Chocolate Factory –1971)

2001

a space ode and ditty

*This book is dedicated to my all my friends
both real and imaginery.*

Colin J Davies

"Look! It's moving. It's alive. It's alive... It's alive, it's moving, it's alive, it's alive, it's alive, it's alive, IT'S ALIVE! Oh, in the name of God! Now I know what it feels like to be God!"[1]

And then my mother said "That's great doctor but, can I hold my baby now."

Late December 1970, and a new geek is born. My name is Colin Davies, and I am a fan. I love horror, sci-fi and fantasy. To be honest I'm not keen on reality. I find the real world lacks the kind of humanity I'm used to reading about in books and comics; it misses the general moral code I find in TV shows and movies; reality seems to, in no way, teach us how to be better people.

The following poems and stories are based on my life as a fan, my loves as a fan, and it all started with a mother's promise:

For the Love of Geek (part one)

Breathe on
You shall feel love
And what dreams may come
Shall be blessed
For you are loved
And will always be
No matter what

Find your own happiness
Seek a world to accept you
And what interests may fall
Shall be encouraged
For you are loved
And we shall always seek to help
No matter what

You have our permission
To find yourself

70ˢ

The 70s

Let me explain my family unit. There was me, the youngest; my brother, the eldest; my mother, the stay at home mum with occasional part time job leading to full time once I was old enough to lose a key, and my father, the breadwinner.

My mum and dad had recently moved to Brighton from Manchester, with my big brother in tow when I can along. A one bedroom flat with a black and white TV in the corner of the sitting room, a set of bunk beds and a cat: this was my first abode.

It was that black and white TV that introduced me to the Doctor. I genuinely cannot remember a time when *Doctor Who* wasn't a major part of my life. This is backed up with photographic evidence. Christmas 1973 and I received the Denys Fisher *War of the Daleks* board game. I had apparently asked Father Christmas for it.

Judging by the look on my face in that picture, I was one very excited 3 year old. Though nowadays, with the small moving parts involved I would have had to have been 8 and above to be allowed to play with such a thing.

Another image burned into my neurons by the gray-scale screen of the black and white TV is of a man fighting a real horned dinosaur. Many years later I found out that the film in question was the 1960 fantasy adventure *The Lost World* directed by Irwin Allen.

It doesn't matter how many times I see that film in colour, the lasting image of the 'real monster' in all it's glorious monochromic detail is far greater than the reality of the dodgy special effects.

They took real lizards and glued bits on them to make them into dinosaurs, turning a gecko in to a baby T-Rex and a young crocodile into a triceratops. Yet in my mind, when I drift back to watching it through the gap in the furniture (due to decorating our bunk beds were in the front room) those dinosaurs are every bit as real as the ones Phil Tippett[2] allowed to run amok when under his supervision in 1993.

Even though the special effects were nowhere near the amazing quality of the mighty Ray Harryhausen, this footage of pimped up geckos and modified iguanas would be used over and over in various TV projects like *Land of the Giants*, *Lost in Space*, *The Time Tunnel* and *Voyage to the Bottom of the Sea*.

This was an age of only three TV channels. No video. No twenty-four hour TV. Films would rerun at the cinema for years in an attempt to gain a new audience and squeeze every last penny out of an idea. I would walk around town holding my mother's hand and being mesmerised by the poster for *Frankenstien* (1931) as we past the Duke of York[3] cinema in Brighton; this would have been about 1974-75.

In the Summer of 1976, I was 5 and my brother was 8. My parents had managed to get a move to a two bedroom council flat in Hollingbury high up on the South Downs north of Brighton. Radio Rentals delivered our first colour TV set and snooker became one of the most amazing things you could ever hope to see.

My father borrowed a book from the library: *A Pictorial History of Horror Movies*. It was full of the most wonderful pictures from Universal, Hammer and other greats including *The Exorcist* and *The Texas Chainsaw Massacre*. It was crammed full of images that fuelled our imaginations.

This was the mid 70s. We hadn't had the gift of *Star Wars* yet. *Jaws* was only round the corner. And none of these films had been shown on TV. All we had was this book, *A Pictorial History of Horror Movies*, and we were fascinated by the pictures. *Dracula, Frankenstein, The Creature from the Black Lagoon*. We would play games of *The Wolfman*, yet we had never seen the film and had no real idea how the story went.

When the BBC started showing these classic films as *the horror double bill* on BBC 2 our excitement had no boundaries; Tom Baker was *Dr Who* and all those creatures from the pages of 'The Book'were now real and undead on my TV screen, life didn't get much better than this.

Being such a young age meant that I had to strike a deal with my mother to be able to stay up late enough to watch these greats. So I agreed to go to bed directly after Doctor Who, which would have been round 6:30pm. Then come 10 o'clock my parents you wake me up to come and watch the two films.

The next day my dad would sit down with me and my brother to discuss the films. What we liked about them? What we didn't like? What we thought of the special effects? And what we thought of the story?

We grew to appreciate the films on many levels. Seeing through the screen, understanding the art as well as being scared witless by the stories.

Those old black & white films still hold a creepy light to my heart. There invention and simplicity were pure magic.

A Trilogy of Terror

Grey scaled eyes
Half dead with new life
More than a passing thought
As the creator cries
The beauty of his simple violation
Does not understand
And as the people fear the coming change
Man begets man
Death becomes a luxury
And fear the new God

My eyes are wide
My heart is racing
My thoughts are fierce
My breath is shallow

Now I see the master
He who defies God
Gorging on the black blood of innocents
Moving across centuries
To find a forgotten promise
Made with a blackened heart
Music of wolves sings to thee
With a sweeping shadow you hide
As the sun delivers warmth
You sleep

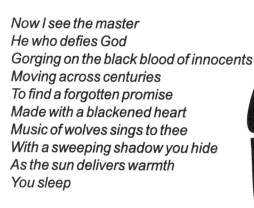

My eyes are wet
My heart is full
My thoughts are deep
My breath is held

Palm devoid of colour
Shows the symbol to prove
That the dog bite was cursed
Tension builds in waiting
The coming of the new moon
Transformed to neither man nor beast
A lycan in haunched silhouette
Peace can only be found with silver
And the hand of one
Who truly loves you

My eyes are lost
My heart is pounding
My thoughts are scattered
My breath is still

The horror double bills gave us more than just Universal, we also got to see the wonderful Technicolor of Hammer. To us the different versions for *Dracula* were just weeks apart, not years. And even though I loved the site of black blood flowing under the door in *Cat People* (1942), directed by Jacques Tourneur, Hammer's Kensington Gore had its own charm.

I find it funny now to think that even though I was a fan of Bela Lugosi, it was the Hammer vampires that sparked my imagination. Not just Christopher Lee, they all had a certain something about them, especially the women.

For years I thought that, should I ever became a vampire, the only people I could feed on would be women with buxom breasts squeezed into a dresses two sizes too small; a huge heaving bosom. Yeah. That's what vampire victims and female vampires looked like to me.

There is a certain romance in the violence of vampires that the Hammer films are drenched in.

Together in Blood

Fall into my eyes
Feel yourself connect
I brush my fingers against your flushed cheek
Then take what I require

Feel my bite
Deep in your vein
I bathe in the blood you hold so dear
And wash my cold flesh

Offer me your soul
For it is yours to give
I shall feast upon you with a hunger
That shall never be satisfied

Hold me tight
As your last daylight breath leaves
I watch your bosom fall still
Silence of the dead

Drink my blood
Feel your own hunger grow
I wince as you greedily suckle on my wrist
Sharing my power

Become my concubine
Give your body freely
I shall give you all that you need to survive
As lovers in the howling wind

Before I move on from the 70s I have to mention *Star Wars*. It changed everything, as *The Exorcist* gave rise to supernatural thrillers; *Star Wars* gave us some of the most amazing cinematic moments we could ever wish for. Not just in its own celluloid but also in the films it inspired like *Close Encounters of the Third Kind*, *Alien* and *The Cat from Outer Space*.

Yes, the story of a humble humidity farmer from a long, long time ago in a galaxy far, far away set a bandwagon in motion that every major studio (and many not so major production companies) wanted to jump on.

There have been so many books, blogs and papers written about the original *Star Wars* trilogy that I was unsure what I could add to the conversation. So I decided to pay tribute to the *Star Wars* films (well the original three) with some Force-inspired limericks.

I didn't just want to write theme pieces, I wanted real attachment, something to show how much these films mean without writing yet another homage. To achieve this I made sure that each piece finishes with an actual line from each of the movies.

There Once was an Original Trilogy

Star Wars[4]
By accident Luke Skywalker Saw
A message on R2's Recorder
But to get off the planet
Old Ben used his magic
"These aren't the droids you're looking for"

The Empire Strikes Back
Old Ben's ghost said "to become a Jedi
To master Yoda it is you must fly
Then Han turned up
Spilled the Tauntaun guts
"I thought they smelled bad on the outside"

Return Of The Jedi
The feeling of anger you can't hide
Your destiny will not be denied
But on this Death Star
Your feeble skills are
"No match for the power of the dark side."

Even though the films are amazing, it was the toys that were the real phenomenon. I can still remember the day I got my first *Star Wars* toy, a C3P0 from Hamleys in Hove (actually). My brother was at his Cub Scout camp and we were buying him a little something for when we visited later that day. It was an incredible drawing kit that consisted of a number of plastic discs with numbers round the edge and numbered lines cut out in the middle section. You set number 1 towards the top of the page, stuck a pin in the centre and drew the line marked number 1. Then you rotated it so that the number 2 was at the top, drawing in line number 2, and so on. Then, when you finished the last line, you took the wheel off the paper and 'TaDa!' there was a Spiderman, or a Hulk.

To stop me feeling left out as my brother was getting this piece of magic I got to choose something and there was only one place for me to look: the *Star Wars* wall. At the tender age of 7 years old I would have been standing at about 1.2 metres tall, looking at a wall some 2m high 2.5m wide (about 7 foot by 8 foot). Every spare gap was filled with *Star Wars* figures. There were thousands and thousands of them. That's how I remember it. In the middle of all these alien creature one figure shone, literally. The golden body of C3P0 caught the light and bounced into my eyes. I had never seen anything so shiny. I reached out my hand to point at the droid.

My father asked me if I was sure, "Wouldn't you prefer a Luke Skywalker?" he asked, lowering the farm boy into my view.

We had seen the film at least three times by this point. Back then the cinema was a cheap way to entertain kids on a Sunday afternoon and even though I had hung off every word of the hero I was adamant, here, in this shop, at this moment: there was nothing else in the world I wanted more (well maybe a real K9, but that wasn't happening soon).

The only words I said as we left the shop were, "Thank you,"and, "Can you open it please?"I sat in the back of our Vauxhall Viva transfixed by my new friend. The arms and legs were so stiff I couldn't get them moving for the entire trip. It was like someone had given me the most precious metal in the world made of plastic.

For weeks he never left my pocket. I only took him out when I wanted a look. Soon that became when I wanted to show my friends, then to play with other figures staring in our own versions of films.

He became more than just a humble communications droid fulfilling his part of a Force induced prophecy. He was the centre of my play, my wing man. More than just a toy, he was part of me.

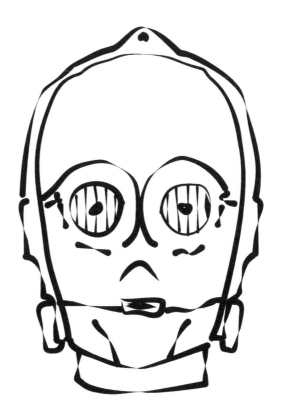

Shiny man

Oh shiny man
Communications droid
Destroyer of worlds
Saviour of lands
God of men
Companion of the Doctor

To me you were everything
All that I could think you to be
Your golden skin reflected more than just light
It showed my thoughts
Throwing back the images of my imagination
As you took on aliens
And werewolves

Oh shiny man
I didn't see you leave
One day I just noticed you were gone
And I searched
In amongst cars
And spaceships
And the shops

I'm sorry I let you down
By letting you go
Without a fight
I miss you
My 3P0

The *Star Wars* phenomena also gave us some great TV and at the end of the 70s, apart from wanting to be travelling with the Jelly Baby addict, the games in the playground with my group of friends focussed on *Blake's 7*.

Now, when you look at it, it's too easy to write off the special effects and low budget sets. But to us, these noble criminals, fighters for free thought and free speech, became our heroes.

We looked up to them and understood their struggle. Even when Blake disappeared and Avon took over the command, the sense of doing the right thing for the people was all too apparent.

I have chosen *Blake's 7* (1978-1981) to end the 70s with a found poem. If you are unaware of this poetry form then let me explain. Found poetry is when you take lines from something verbatim, and reorder them to read like a poem.
So this found poem is made up of things Avon said during all four seasons of the programme. And, what's more, they are in chronological order.

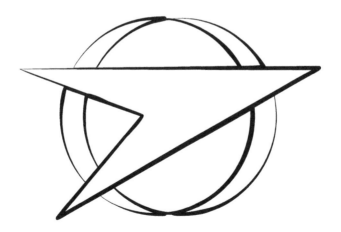

Avon, a found poem[5]

Have you ever met an honest man?
I relied on other people
Don't try to manipulate me
Don't philosophise at me, you electronic moron!
Automatic reaction, I'm as surprised as you are
I'll tell you a fact of life
Change is inevitable!
That's the trouble with heroics,
They seldom run to schedule.
I have never understood why it should be necessary
To become irrational
In order to prove that you care
Logic says we're dead
Another idealist, poor but honest
Shall look forward to our meeting with eager anticipation

Staying with you requires a degree of stupidity
Of which I no longer feel capable
It's the kind of natural stupidity no amount of training
Could ever hope to match
Law makers, law breakers, let us fight them all!

What a very depressing thought.
It is considered ill-mannered to kill your friends
While committing suicide
And alone, probably
Virtually alone, then
Oh, you are curious
You are expendable.
I do not need anybody at all
Locate and destroy it.
The two don't necessarily follow

As far as I'm concerned you can destroy whatever you like
You can stir up a thousand revolutions
You can wade in blood up to your armpits
Oh, and you can lead the rabble to victory
Whatever that may mean
Just so long as there's an end to it.
And I want it finished! I want it over and done with
I want to be free!
I want to be free of him!

I have had enough excitement for a while
Right now a little boredom wouldn't come amiss
It has a perverse kind of logic to it
Surprise seems inappropriate somehow

You should never judge by appearances
I had hoped for a more inspiring epitaph
Too good to become involved with the rest of humanity
Of all the things I am, I never recognized the fool
Make me die. There's nothing else you can make me do
Don't be sorry. Be Quiet

Idealism is a wonderful thing,
All you need is someone rational to put it to proper use
Stand still!
Have you betrayed us?
Have you betrayed me?

The 80s

With the turn of the decade came world awareness. I listened to Pink Floyd's *The Wall* and understood what it was trying to say. I read the *Hitchhikers Guide to the Galaxy*, then watched the TV series, then listen to the rerun of the radio play. My mind was exploding with new ideas and yet, I was still only young.

I watched *The Incredible Hulk*, *Spiderman* and *Wonder Woman*. The low production values meant nothing to me, it was all just perfect. I was also noticing how the people around us had different attitudes to this stuff.

Take my brother, he was and is as much of a geek as I am. You want to talk about *Alien*; he's your man no doubt. He was also the sporty one. In America he would have been a jock. He loves football, lives for it; as much as he lives for Bond movies and the playstation.

I'm the same just not so athletic. Back in the day our friends were very different. With all his sporting buddies there was no way he could admit to being a massive *Batman* fan. Whereas I, in my circle of Hobbit-loving sci-fi nerds, would have had my membership card ripped up in front of me had I expressed my rather strong interest in football.

So, as kids we lived in different worlds, only at home, and now in possession of a video recorder, did we ever indulge in our shared interests.

Crossing the boundaries between fantasy and reality is something most children can do with little effort, though becoming your heroes was sometimes a very dangerous affair.

My mother had a friend on the estate called Pet, a fierce looking woman who only took on the form of a human female when she was going out on the pull. She had been moved by the council on account that her daughter, Sarah, had got to that age when things began to change and she 'required' her own room, or at least a separate room from her 7 year old brother Jason.

The new house wasn't that far from the flats so one day towards the end of the summer holidays in 1981, me and my mum walked down to see them. While those two had a coffee and a catch up chat I went up stairs to play.

Sarah was far too mature to play with a 10 year boy like me. She went off to sit in her room and do whatever it was that 11 year old girls do, like learning passages about the Goblin King or something. Jason appeared in the hall, he was playing in the most mysterious and dangerous place any child could ever try the find entertainment, his mother's bedroom. Accompanied by an *Action Man* I entered with a sense of trepidation.

Being naughty always added a certain ambience to any situation, make that naughtiness the occupation of the forbidden zone, and the atmosphere becomes palatable.

I cautiously studied the room. My *Action Man* used his eagle eyes to scan the corners for hidden enemy agents. Jason, obviously not feeling the same sense of foreboding leapt onto the bed. Using the extra spring of the mattress he propelled himself on to the wooden chest of drawers. This put him in the perfect position to continue his ascent onto the top of the 1950s tallboy wardrobe.

The ceiling wasn't high enough for him to stand. By the way he crouched on the edge you could see that this was not the first time he had been in the position. Before I could draw breath Jason

yelled, "Wonder Woman!" and launched himself towards the bed.
I think his over-eagerness to show off in front of me caused his miscalculation. Instead of hitting the sweet spot on the soft mattress he fell short, crashing into the floor and banging his arm against the foot of the heavy wooden frame.

With my limited medical knowledge and by the pitch of his screams, I could tell his arm was broken. My instincts kicked in: first shout for mum, check; second, realise you are going to get in to trouble, check; third, start to cry, check.

The two mothers came charging up the stairs. Pet was shouting warning as she moved to instil fear in us youngster, like when the Americans play *Ride of the Valkyries* before bombing the crap out of the enemy in Vietnam.

"You better not be in my room!"

Fear turns to panic. As the adults enter the room, the emotions are at such a high state that speech has become almost impossible. My mother went over to attend to Jason. Pet got hold of my shoulders and started to shake me with every syllable she shouted.

"What happened here?"

I don't know how much you know about children who have got to such a level of fear and general upsetness where their words become a drone, and drool falls from their mouths like ectoplasm, but you can take it from me, shaking them does not help.

Sarah came into the room. Mum instructed her to go to the phone in the hall and dial 999. Pet stopped shaking me for a second as the instructions were given, then she returned to her interrogation.

"What happened here?" Her line of questioning still wasn't working.

Suddenly Jason stopped crying of a moment, lifted his head up and spoke.

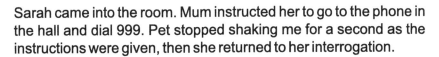

"I was being Wonder Woman."

A moment of silence fell. Then as soon as he started screaming again Pet's shaking strategy continued

"Why was he being Wonder Woman?"

Eventually the ambulance arrived and poor Jason was taken to hospital. Sarah came back to our place while he was being fixed. We sat in mine and my brother's bedroom playing records and reading *2000AD*. Turned out she quite liked sci-fi. Soon the call came and my dad drove her home.

As years pass you lose touch with people, for no other reason than things just change. A few years back I was visiting my friends in Brighton. I was running a bit early so I took a slight detour to drive past the old estate. I popped into the ASDA in Hollingbury to get some snacks.

I was looking at some fruit in the produce section; I had no intention of buying any I just like to look at something healthy before going on to buy large amounts of crisps. I got a tap on the shoulder, when I turned round I saw a woman standing, smiling at me. She looked about my age, vaguely familiar, I just couldn't place her.

"Are you Colin?" she asked

"Yes." It was very obvious that I had no idea who she was.

"I'm Diana," she smiled. "You used to know me as Jason."

Even now when I think back on that meeting I get a slight tear in my eye. Turns out he really did want to be Wonder Woman, even took on her name. So it may have been cheesy acting, poor scripts and lousy effects, but it helped that young boy become the woman she wanted to be.

When I Grow Up

Many moons ago
A teacher said to me
Tell me boy, when you grow up
What do you want to be?

Is it a fireman?
Or a sailor?
A train driver perhaps?
Or Lion Tamer
In the circus
Wearing your new Lion Tamer's hat?

Or a policeman
With a truncheon
Catching bad guys on the run?
Or a military man in the army
With a trade and a shooting gun?

I look at him, tilted head
I swear that this is true
I said "I don't want to be any of those things.
I want to be Doctor Who."

So you can keep your poxy fire truck
Though I'm sure it's really exciting
And to sail upon the seven seas
Is actually quite inviting

And soldiers and coppers with batons and guns
Wearing their clodhopper boots
Do nothing to ping my slightest interest
I want to be Doctor Who

I could be Superman flying around
With my big red flapping cape

Or Spiderman slinging swings abound
With responsibilities great

Batman has always been a favourite of mine
Oh and the Incredible Hulk too
But none of them can travel through time you see
I want to be Doctor Who

To fly around the universe
In Time And Relative Dimensions In Space
Saving civilizations from tyrannies amass
To never die, only change your face

Understanding the beauty of the most violent of creatures
Traveling in your small box of blue
There's nothing on this earth to compare
I want to be Doctor Who

The teacher was not pleased with this
And told me if I wanted to survive
Pay my bills and have a good life
"You need to get a 9 to 5."

I could not argue with this statement
The concept was nothing new
But he asked me, what I wanted to be
And I wanted to be Doctor Who

From that day on I've always worked hard
Made enough cash to do as I please
Though I have never tamed any lions
Or driven any trains from A to B

I've always stayed friends with the superheroes
I first met when I was at school
And every weekend when my son is Peter Pan
I am Doctor Who

The 80s were also where I started playing something that would become a major part of my life: role playing games. It all started because my friend Dylan, during the Easter holidays of '2, bought a rule book for *RuneQuest*. So with Dylan as the Games Master and his brother Shane as a fellow player, we rolled up a couple of characters and tried it out.

From the first session we were hooked. We were 11 at the time and, as I've said before, the ability to step sideways into another universe was easy.

I stopped playing when we went up to high school in '3 and then my family moved from the estate to a house in the middle of Brighton in 1984. Before I realised it a couple of years had passed.

I needed some stuff for my school work and thought I'd use it as an excuse to go and see my old friend. I knocked on the door in the hope he was in. Luckily he was. We got chatting about stuff and it turned out he had carried on role playing and had a new group. We discussed the game for a while before he showed me the rules for the game they were playing, a space opera called *Traveller*. It was amazing stuff.

He told me of his intention to start up another *RuneQuest* game and asked if I would be interested in helping him create the world. We spent weeks building a little village called *Blossom*. Each house had a secret and evil was never to far away. I still remember the excitement we had coming up with ideas that, in truth and by the nature of role playing games may never have been ever found by the players. One I was proud of was the potter.

He made all the crockery used in the village and had the most beautiful daughter, Areila. Only she wasn't real. He made her from clay then struck a deal with a demon to turn her into a real girl, with this proviso.

"Though should she ever find out her true self, or should any man have knowledge of her as a woman, then the spell shall be broken and to clay she shall return."

We were 15, and this was like yes! It would be near on seventeen years before this secret was discovered. I had moved to Blackpool in 1988 and was unaware that they were still playing in the universe until one day in 2003 the death threats started.

The character Cail, was somewhat upset to find that after making romantic advances on a woman he loved more than the gods, she suddenly turned to a clay statue around his penis. Dylan, in a vain attempt to try and appease him, explained that it wasn't him but me who wrote that little gem.

Matt, the player, eventually got my phone number and after a break of too many years our friendship bonded again. But from a safe distance at first: I'm still convinced he's plotting something.

It does go to show how much these games affect our lives. They are not just silly little games, they are fully realised, living things. Recently I visited Matt in London. The reason I gave to my better half for the trip was that we were getting together to write some comedy sketches. The real reason was that Dylan was also going to be there and I was going to join in on the campaign and play the dwarf character I had created for our first ever game.

We regularly meet up online to play smaller skirmish stylized games in the Traveller universe using video conferencing and *table top* software.

The next piece is based on actual events from a *Traveller* game. This was my first ever session with this new group. I had been writing for them for a while, but this was the first time we had played together. It was an unusual game night for the fact that Chris was taking the session as GM (Games Master) instead of Dylan.

My Forty Second Character

In teenage dreams
He was born
Rolled on a Tuesday afternoon
When school was done

Just me, my GM and the Traveller's rules
Working hard to make him realistic
Skills giving him plenty of depth
Backed by characteristics

After two and a half hours
He was ready to be seen
Like David Bowie one eye was blue
The other was green

And so it comes
The first mission's a go
New crew to meet
New face to show

With a quick greeting
We head away from this earth
For travelling the long journey ahead
We are placed in Low Berth

The outer planet is reached
But before a plan can be laid
To come out of Low Berth
A roll must be made

At thirty-eight years
My skill list is long
I could back flip out of the deep freeze
Pulling out both my guns
Summersault over the guards

While hacking the computer with one hand
Rewriting the entire communications system
To use a hidden high frequency band

I could drop kick an Imperium spy
Right in the nuts
Then using my ample medic skills
I'd fix the rest of my party's cuts

Having a mature character
Gives you so much more
Now roll those two D six
Get that high score

Frozen moment locked in time
As the dice roll out of my fingers
A wry smile of future success
The joy of life lingers

Two D six hit the floor, bounce and settle
Counting the dots of success
Everything changes
Snakes eyes stare back at me without blinking

Not just a fail
Botched!
Someone opened the fridge door
But the light did not come on
Gone!

Sat in stasis
I gaze upon the corpse of David Branstien
Thirty-eight years lived
Forty-two seconds played

In forty-two seconds I discover
The meaninglessness of life
The universe and everything
Gone!

I hear nothing around me
Transfixed by the double one
Two little dots
I swear I heard the cat laugh
Gone!

Distant echoes become voices
Mumbles become words
Back in the room
The best character I'd ever had
Didn't come out of fucking Low Berth

He was the second character
I had ever created
To have life with a player
In the game

My first; a dwarf
Explored Rune Quest *landscapes*
And is still alive
To this day

I've lost at least
Three Barbarians, one vampire and three trolls
Since my forty-second character
From this mortal coil did fall

Yet it is the brightest flame
With the shortest life
That remains my biggest regret of them all
And if I ever meet the chap responsible
For writing those Low Berth rules
I'll swiftly drop kick him
A double one
Right into his crown jewels

The bastard!

I can't talk about the 80s without mentioning the 'Video Nasty'; or the bad movies with plenty of gore to be more accurate.

Role-playing got a bad rep because two people who liked *Dungeons & Dragons* killed some people. The same witch-hunt happened with low budget (yet highly imaginative) horror films. One nutjob did something bad. He also liked *A Texas Chainsaw Massacre,* ergo the gory film made him hurt those people.

The fact that Tobe Hooper's classic tale of inbred cannibalistic country folk is a true feat of film making, with far reaching themes that will go on to become clichés in the genre carries no weight; the murdering bastard liked it, it must be evil.

Of course there were some that have very little artistic merit and were just plain nasty. *The Night of the Demon* was one of those. Not to be confused with the classic British horror film from 1957 directed by Jacques Tourneur. This film from 1980 directed by James C Wasson involved a professor taking his students into the woods in search of Bigfoot. What they found was black magic, and a man in a black hairy suit who then began to kill everyone.

I knew I was onto a winner in the video shop because the cover was just a blank case with *Night of the Demon* written in blue ballpoint on a ripped off piece of paper. Yes, I thought it was the original. But, when I put it into the video player (that we got from Harry the Bastard) what I saw was a biker getting his cock ripped off when he stops by the roadside to have a wee. And a very strange final scene which involved the hair mutation pulling out some guy's intestines and swinging them round his head for no apparent reason.

These were the days when me and my brother, and by default our parents, would devour three to four films a night. Like I said, we only had three channels; the fourth hadn't come online by this point. This was where I first got to see *The Exorcist (1973)*, *The Texas Chainsaw Massacre (1974)*, *Night of the Living Dead* (1968) and so many more from *A Pictorial History of Horror Movies*.

I got to watch a head explode in *Turkey Shoot* (1982) directed by Brian Trenchard-Smith, a film about criminals sent to a torturous prison camp and offered freedom if they become the prey in a human hunt for VIP guests; I witnessed cannibals fighting over the guts of a recently sliced open explorer in *Cannibal Holocaust (1980)* directed by Ruggero Deodato, which is the first movie to use the now popular 'found footage' style and I had the pleasure of seeing eyes gouged out by zombies and people eaten by flesh eating spider in *The Beyond (1981)* directed by Lucio Fulci.

These blood soaked video cassettes were gruesome yet highly entertaining. The low budget qualities added to the fun and I was more fascinated in how they achieved the effect than I was in thinking ripping someone's guts out was actually a really good idea.

Ode to the Video Nasty

Bloody, blood spills over the knife
An eye pierced by a spike
Broken fingers, broken necks
He's ripped out her throat, my God what next?

Nails pulled, skulls crushed
Cannibals fighting to eat some guy's guts
Zombies drooling after the brains of the living
Everyone's dying after a murderous Thanksgiving

School killer slasher madmen
Victimised so they come back again
To reap revenge on the now grown bullies
By hanging their skinned corpses from a system of pulleys

Demons, maniacs, zombies and ghouls
Monsters that eat the souls of the moral-less fools
Backpackers, students, professors and police
All meet a sticky end in this nasty video feast.

There was some great sci-fi in the 80s. *E.T The Extra Terrestrial* came to our screens and ripped our hearts apart. It was also the first really big pirated film. I still maintain that the absolutely unwatchable quality of those illegal tapes made more people go to the cinema to watch it so instead of hurting the box office it actually increased it.

From dying aliens covered in flour to one of the greatest trilogies of all time. *Back to the Future*, a series of films that captured the vibe of the time so well you felt like you were part of the story, watching it again after so many years transports you back to the 80s, so in a way it has become a time travelling device.

I still get the hairs on the back of my arm standing on end when Marty and Jennifer kiss in front of the clock tower and Huey Lewis's slightly strained voice comes in with, "That's the power of love,"before the rest of the News continue with that killer riff.

Ridley Scott gave us *Blade Runner,* and allowed us to think of a future that wasn't all shiny and *Star Trek II* re-acquainted us with the wonderfully villainous Khan.

Tobe Hooper made a come back to horror with *Poltergeist.* I know, a lot of people think it's a Spielberg film as they do with Joe Dante's *Gremlins* (my favourite Christmas movie) and Richard Donner's *The Goonies.*

Out of all the amazing fantasy films like *Labyrinth, Krull* and *Beast Master,* my personal favourite is (and for my money the only true high fantasy film ever made because it contains no humans at all), *The Dark Crystal*: A tale of good and evil. light and dark, Mystics and Skeksis; With the last two Gelflings, Jen and Keria, predicted to bring unison over the lands once more.

Growing up in the 80s as a fan was amazing. We had all the 70s shows repeating, and an incredible choice of newly released films that would become classic, remember, I haven't even mentioned *Ghostbusters.*

This was the decade comic books became literature. *The Dark Knight Returns* had taken the classic hero and added the gritty realism that comics like *2000AD* had introduced a generation to. This was followed by *Watchmen* and *Killing Joke*. Suddenly the comic was less childish and more of a threat to the establishment. This is typified with the publication of *V for Vendetta*.

With *Doctor Who* slowly being killed off by budget cuts, the graphic novels became a source of ideas and moral teaching. Taking us on journeys that twisted the established order and subverted our understanding of what a hero really was.

Drawn is the Story

Ink to frame
And back again
In universes parallel
The ghost sits on the carousel
And rides the lifeless horse
That brings us to our main course

Laugh the Joker said crying
As bat is to night
I shall be the dawn
Son of Jor-El
Let this be known

Let the government fear thy people
As the Crow sits on the steeple
The Watchmen become less feeble
Politics is explained in exaggerated caricature
That is close enough to the truth
To be dangerous

Time to fold the faces
Close the book
This lesson is over
So take another look

As a fan I often use lines from films or TV programmes as actual speech. Back in the 80s me and my friends would have whole conversations using nothing but quotes, usually from James Cameron's 1986 *Alien* sequel *Aliens*.

This is a found poem from within the dialogue of this wonderful movie.

Aliens, a found poem[6]

Hey Vasquez
Have you ever been mistaken for a man?
This little girl survived …with no weapons and no training.
Why don't you put her in charge?
Just deal with it, because…I'm sick of your bullshit
They cut the power
I don't know which species is worse
How do I get out of this chickenshit outfit?
He can't make that kind of decision. He's just a grunt!
It'll be dark soon, and they mostly come at night
You don't see them fucking each other over for a goddamn percentage
Hey man, I don't wanna rain on your parade
I like to keep this hand... for close encounters
What the hell are we supposed to use man? Harsh language?
Get away from her, you bitch!
I may be synthetic, but I'm not stupid
Stop your grinnin' and drop your linen!
I say we take off and nuke the entire site from orbit
It's the only way to be sure
That's it, man. Game over, man! Game over!
What the fuck are we gonna do now?

The 90s

1990, the second Summer of love was in full flow in the North of England and had been since 1989. Ecstasy was not illegal yet, acid house was the choice of ravers everywhere and *Akira* was having a one off midnight showing at the ABC in Blackpool.

I had already seen the film on laserdisc the year before, but the largest screen you could easily get back then was a 28" So this was my chance to see this amazing piece of art on the big screen.

I managed to talk my friend Mick into coming along by using the skills I had learned from being a high end Hi-Fi salesman.

I said, "Do you want to come and see Akria?"

And he said, "Yeah. Alright."

We sat in the pub across the road from the cinema. A few pints in here, a quarter bottle of vodka mixed into a litre of Coke and a couple of happy pills for good measure. All bases covered.

While we were enjoying the early part of the evening we got talking to a couple of girls. They were dressed from the scene, bright eyes, bright coloured clothes, and bright personalities. Everything was cool. Both me and Mick were on such comic form that night that these girl actually asked *us* out. They were heading off to a rave club followed by a minibus to a field just outside Blackburn.

I looked over at the cinema. Suddenly I had a choice to make. Do I go and join the collective, drop my everyday face and find solace in the combined humanity of conjoined pleasure. A bliss-filled night full of colour and sound shared with like minded people all there to expand their personal horizons enwrapped in the warm hug of over welling excitement, ROOOOBAARRRBS! Or do we go to a nightclub and rave with these girls.

By the time I met my partner Heather in '1, I had already been to a fair few raves both night club and field based. However, still to this day I've only ever seen *Akria* at the cinema once. I'm pretty sure those girls had a great night without us.

On the Edge of Colour

Otomo, I ride with the Capsules
Free spirits in an oppressed world
Feeling the wind in my hair
The power beneath me
Two wheels propelling my body
Through the streets of Neo-Tokyo

My powers are great
Akira awakens
Otomo, you give me such colours
As to evoke the second creation
As the ever-expanding universe
Of another dimension
Is started with a single uttered thought
I am Tesuo

Vampires came to mean a lot to me in the 90s. I had been writing some stories for the role playing game *Vampire: the Masquerade* with Iayn, a new friend of mine that I had met through the hi-fi store. Later on I would join the group he GM'd and start playing in his dark vision of London nightlife.

Interview with the Vampire became a must see movie, and of course *Buffy the Vampire Slayer* and *Angel* became Friday nights in front of the TV.

The beautiful people via evil, this series hit the right chord almost channelling the time. Like *Back to the Future* it perfectly captures the moment in history without being topical. Each new story would combine horror, comedy and real issues regarding growing up and identity. Clever writing, superb acting and great special FX all combined to create an amazing piece of television

But in this genre-busting TV show one question was always being asked...

Who would you do in Buffy?
(a man's/lesbian's perspective)

Oh Buffy, sweet Buffy
You're really pretty and all
And given half the chance,
I'd certainly step out with you for sure

But the other one is so much sexier
As far as the Slayers compare
So given the choice, I would rather have Faith
I also know that Spike's not been there.

Anya's a bit of alright
And Cordelia's full of playfulness
But they both strike me as very needy
And that makes them high maintenance

Now Buffy's sister the key
Is sweet that's for sure
But she's way too young to be discussed
So we'll leave that one at the door

There is one girl in the Buffyverse
And here is the reveal
I'd crawl over broken glass to be with her
Especially when she was evil

Those blackened eyes and ancient powers
Oh Willow you are the one for me
Please take my soul, take my heart
And I will worship thee.

And your girlfriend wasn't too shabby either.

The Doctor came back to visit me briefly in1986 before kissing his companion and disappearing for another nine years (officially). Heading towards the end of the decade the realisation that this was now going to be the end of the century was becoming clear.

Strange thoughts filled my head like: what will they call *2000AD*? According to all the programmes, films and comics, we were heading very quickly towards the future and we still didn't have a base on the moon.

The hope given to us by geniuses like Gerry Anderson; that there was more to this universe, to this planet, had been given a new assertion by *The X-Files* with its true conspiracies about aliens and governments.

The millennium bug was about to destroy everything by launching all the nuclear weapons. Maybe this was how we were going to get the *Cursed Earth.*

Through my mid to late 20s I was beginning to lose faith in what up until now had been my hope. OK films like *The Crow, The Fifth Element* and *Jurassic Park* filled me with much joy. I was starting to be amazed by the way they looked, not what they were saying to me about things to come.

I did find solace with the Sony Playstation. *Resident Evil,* and in particular *Silent Hill,* both scared me witless through some tough times. As the millennium approached my cynicism had started to grow.

Peace: As The Crow Dies

I walk along
With you in my mind
Obsessed

My love for you
Drives me to live on
Beyond death

I refuse to die
To have my revenge
You bet

Don't look the crow cries
But I see them
They're next

I can't sleep till
The debt is paid up
All dead

And as the flesh
Rots from my bones
Don't fret

It has come to an end
Together again
Now rest

Y2K

So the clock passed midnight and nothing changed. The bombs did not go off, the planes did not fall out of the sky and the corned beef did not explode. Nothing changed. And I was bitterly disappointed.

Y2K - What future?

Robots
I wanted robots
Big, strong shiny machines
To help me do stuff and carry things
Where are my robots?

Jumpsuits
Silver jumpsuits
For walking around bases on the moon
Practical, durable and cool
What happen to my silver jumpsuits?

Space
Holidays in space
Going up in a rocket to a space station hotel
With views from your window of the curvature of our world
Why can't I holiday in space?

I want a future with space suits not onesies
I want a tomorrow with Easy Rocket not Jet 2
I want to live alongside androids and computers
I want to have laser guns and light sabres coz they're cool

I felt lied to by my comics and films
I thought Space 1999 *would become true*
The future was here becoming the present
And it felt like nothing new.

By the end of the year 2000 I had turned 30, everything I had hoped for from my love of all things geek had not or did not look like becoming reality.

Then in February 2001 we were told our father was ill. He died in the March listening to *Dark Side of the Moon* by Pink Floyd.

Goodbye Dad

From the time that they gave you,
There was nothing much that you could do
Scared sitting on the sofa
Wondering when
It will be over

And as Pink sang Black and Blue
There was nothing left for you to do
But to let go of the shell
You'd occupied
Since Hitler fell

And they put you in a bag
Then they put you in a box
And they shoved you in a car
With mourners gathered
Like some street bazaar

We carried you inside
The velvet curtain used to hide
And the mood was very sullen
Mother read the Lord's Prayer
They fired up the oven

Ashes to Ashes
And Funk to Funky
A stone with your name on
In a field
With other lost sons

Now life has a Dad-shaped hole
Which loving cancer left for us all
Memories make the void arbitrary
In this life
That is momentary.

And in that moment everything became real. It felt like my entire world had been taken away. The future I was promised hadn't arrived; I had lost a barbarian character I really liked, this time because of some stupid rules involving bleeding and the prospect of hover boards becoming a reality in the next fourteen years looked like a pipe dream. The death of our father was just too much reality.

I started obsessing about the bad things that had happened in the past. The cruelty I had witnessed on the estate as a child. Not in our home, but in the homes of my friends.

I felt I had a trapped memory, something so bad I was scared of it. Comic books, role playing game, films, they all meant nothing. I had convinced myself that my love for these was because I used to use them to hide in: to not face the horrors of the estate.

I decided that the only way to deal with this was to go back and face my demons. So in the September 2001 I travelled down south. There was only one person who could have been there for this pilgrimage and that was my oldest friend, and first GM, Dylan.

It was a beautiful sunny day. We walked through our old school grounds then up through the estate; walking the streets we used to play in. As we trod these old tarmac paths all the memories of mucking about in the fields, climbing onto the roofs and running amok came flooding back.

We'd worked our way up to the last row of flats before the farmer's field. There I saw a wall, not just any wall, but the first wall.

I entered my mind TARDIS and travelled back to 1981.

2000AD ran a two part Judge Dredd story called *UnAmerican Graffiti* (prog 206 –207). We all got our copy of the comic on the Saturday and read the first part. It was awesome. There was this graffiti tagger called Chopper who was trying to be the best in Mega

City One by tagging (writing his graffiti name) on the highest point. But every time he had placed a new tag his rival, Phantom, would scrawl just above it.

On the Sunday I was playing out with Dylan when I picked up a lump of chalk and wrote on this wall CHOPPER, with a smiley face in the O. It made us laugh. We went home as normal; went to school like any other Monday. Came home, got changed and went out to play. There, on the wall, just above where I had written 'CHOPPER' someone had scrawled 'Phantom' with the ghost outline.

This was the start of something that became known locally as the 'chalk wars' For the next week I was trying to write CHOPPER as high as I could, and so was the mysterious Phantom; with his tag of course.

Saturday came and with it the concluding second part which revealed that 'Phantom' was in fact *Spoiler Alert* a painting droid. We were shocked and applauded such a twist that none of us saw coming.

On the Sunday, the Phantom from the 'chalk wars' was also unmasked as none other than our good friend Tony Hamlin. The rest of the summer was spent writing on every bit of wall we could find.

Some old geezer complained to the local Bobby about the vandalism. We all had a bit of a giggle when he was informed that it was only chalk and it would wash off when it rained.

Ditching the mind TARDIS for the mind DeLorean, I drove back to the present, and there I was, in front of wall zero. That was the memory I was scared of. Not so much the 'chalk wars' but the fun we had as kids. With everything that had happened I had forgotten how much fun we had. In that instant I had an epiphany, it was 2001 and this was my monolith moment.

All the sci-fi, fantasy and horror I loved use to represent the future. The films I could see when I was old enough; prediction of times to come; ideals of a better life. Now I realised it was all about seeing the past; these films, TV shows, books, computer games are all about getting that feeling back, of being the child again.

My Kingdom

I once commanded armies
Of Trolls and Orcs and men
Ten thousand strong legions
I fought alongside them

We fought in bloody battles
For love and righteous song
Saving the princess from the black knight
With valour we righted wrong

I stood up against the vampire master
Severed the wolverine blood line
Built a monster out of man's spare parts
Drew the seventh sign

I had the power and the wealth
That only man can dare to dream
I saw the beauty in the universe
That still is yet unseen

I had it in the palm of my hand
I want it back again
Watching over my kingdom
When I was only ten

It all made sense, I found my joy again. All those feelings of wide eyed wonder that had been slowly chipped away with the pressures of growing up, that magic sparkle whose light had been dimmed with responsibilities, that sense of hope that had been ripped away when the promise of the future had fail to materialise; they all came back.

Suddenly I was free from the burden of anticipation. I understood what my mum and dad had been telling us all these years, that to be who you are is to be happy. I am a geek, as is my brother, and as was our father.

It is such a shame that I am unable to thank our dad for this gift. But through the eyes of my son, through his relationship with his uncle and grandma, through the love bestowed upon him from our friends: the best way I can thank our dad is to teach the next generation the same important lessons.

Trust yourself, let others be themselves and just be you. Don't change to fit, find friends that fit. Allow those around you to love you. It's not about escaping from the world; it's about being part of a world.

For the Love of Geek (part two)

You made me who I am today
Giving me the tools to build
Letting me design my own paths
Showing me the map
And letting me plan the route

All the time your were there to catch me
Should I have fallen towards the rocks
Never outwardly judging my decisions
Loving me no matter what
Thank you for showing me Doctor Who
For letting me watch all those films
Defending my right to read what I liked
Never mocking my choice of friends

I felt loved
I am loved
Thank you mum
I love you too

So now we have *Doctor Who* back, new *Star Trek,* new *Star Wars.* Both me and my brother have started getting fit. It's been easier for him because he was always the jock. But he summed it up perfectly as to why we had these changes in attitude towards our health.

"We are getting older, Bro,"he said. "In the next couple of years we've got *Star Wars EP 7*; *Batman vs Superman*; more Marvel films; *Playstation 4*; and a whole host of other stuff. And we want to be around for them coming out."

I also want to add to that the change in the *Doctor Who* canon that has removed the finite number of regeneration. I want to be around for when my grandkids say, "He's not as good as the last one. Oh no. Hang on. He's the best doctor there's ever been."

In realising that my love for all these stories, all these characters are part of me. In accepting that enjoying these films and graphic novels and TV programmes and games makes me happy; in letting myself be that 10 year old boy again (though with a much better understanding of the mysteries of life, like girls and the end of Quantum Leap). In understanding that this is me and those who love me accept this as I accept them for who they are and what they like, I found true happiness. I became my own Diana Prince and instead of trying to fit in, I just let myself be.

Midway through the 2010s and a middle-aged geek shares his stories with the world. I am Colin Davies and I am a fan.

Live long and prosper.

DVD Extra Easter Egg - A Poem for Sean Payne

Of Swords and Sorcery

Come to me companions
Come to me from far
Follow me into battle
To beat my evil brother

For he has killed our father
And slain my sweet beloved
So to stop his reign of tyranny
My brother must be dead

Come join me in the fight
Come stand with me forever
And we shall free the Abbess
For I am Hawk the Slayer

DVD Extra - Notes

1. Quote taken from the 1931 version of Frankenstein directed by James Whale, Written by (play) Peggy Webling – (Adaptation) John L. Balderston – (Screenplay) Francis Edward Faragoh, Garrett Fort – (novel) Mary Shelley

2. Phil Tippet is a movie director and special effect animator who created the go-motion technique. His works include Star Wars Episode V The Empire Strikes Back, Episode VI Return of the Jedi, Dragon Slayer and the Jurassic Park films. It is on the credits for Jurassic Park that he is given the title of 'Dinosaur Supervisor' which, due to the amount of death and mayhem seen in the film, he is considered bad at his job.

3. Opening in 1910 The Duke of York's cinema was built one of the first purpose built cinemas in the world. Built on the site of the Amber Ale Brewery, Preston Rd, Brighton, by actress-manager Violet Melnitte for a cost of £3000, with the original wall of the brewery used from the rear of the auditorium.

4. Becoming a New Hope when re-released on home video in 1981.

5. Blake's 7 was created by Terry Nation who also created the Daleks for Doctor Who. Writers that may be in this found poem: Chris Boucher; Terry Nation; Allan Prior; Robert Holmes; Roger Parkes; Ben Steed; James Follett; Tanith Lee; Trevor Hoyle; Rod Beacham; Colin Davis; Bill Lyons; Simon Masters

6. Aliens (1986) story by James Cameron, David Giler and Walter Hill based on characters created by Dan O'Bannon and Ronald Shusett. Screenplay by James Cameron.

DVD Extra - Bout the Author

Colin Davies (1970-) was born in Brighton. At the age of 17 he moved to Blackpool where he embarked on a journey to become a successful and highly respected author, poet and playwright.

His second novel for children, *"Mathamagical II: Anagramaphobia - at word's end"* is a 2015 Red Ribbon winner at the Wishing Shelf Book Awards. Colin's solo spoken word show "2001: A Space Ode and Ditty" was short-listed for the 2015 Saboteur show of the year award, placing third.

Colin lives with his partner and son and writes in many different genres and styles, where his love of film, music, poetry and football infuse with his memories of childhood to create wonderful tales.

Colin has sat on the committee of the Lancashire Dead Good Poets' Society. He writes reviews and blog posts for the award-winning websites deadgoodpoets.blogspot.co.uk and altblackpool.co.uk as well as regular updates to his own blog.

He has been instrumental in helping local poets into positions as writers in residence and seeks to help writers advance in their chosen field of art.

DVD Extra - May the 4th Special

This was written for a spoken word night on the 4th of May 2015 at the Eagle Inn in Salford to celebrate all things Star Wars. I wrote it as if Emperor Palpatine was going to a spoken word open mic night. If you try and do his voice in the way Family Guy taught us "Something, something, something, Dark Side" it works really well.

The Emperor's New Poem

*For many years I have taught
Darth Vader to use
The Dark Side of the Force.*

*Channelling the anger
From his youth
Twisting his vision
To see my truth.*

*Power through fear
Strength in evil
Destroying those who oppose me
So that the Dark Side will prevail.*

*Good, I can feel your anger grow
Join us, for you destiny is so
The rebels' stand will end in defeat
And your journey to the Dark Side
Will be complete.*

*I just hope my Storm Troopers
Don't run into those bloody Ewoks
Though little bastards!*

Why would Pi stop Dye Ameter walking more than three times round the table? And why would Mr Ameter do what Pi told him? Ben Small is good at English but rubbish at Mathematics.

Branded a cheat by the headmaster of Cottomwall Grammar School because of the inconsistencies in his test results Ben feels he has no choice but to run away. Due to the storm he beds down for the night in the science lab of his school where, quite by chance, he meets a talking snake called Adder. Hearing Ben's story Adder asks Ben to come with him to MATHAMAGICAL, the city of Maths to help them solve an English problem and stop a war with the Advancing Alphas. Join Ben and Adder as they journey across the mathematical landscapes in their quest to save the numbers.

This charming yet informative children's novel can be read to children as young as 5 and read by all ages. Influenced by *Alice in Wonderland* and the works of *Roald Dahl*, the story follows a young boy and a talking snake travelling from this world to one filled with imagination. Being the world is populated by numbers and mathematical symbols the rules to which they live teaches Ben, the boy and the reader, about basic mathematics ideas without having to do a single sum.

The perfect bedtime story to be enjoyed by the reader and the listener.

ISBN: 978-1471622052

Available on Amazon

The nouns don't know who they are. The verbs have stopped doing anything. And I can't even begin to describe what's happened to the adjectives!

Adder's gone missing, the letters are in trouble and Pi hasn't got a clue what's going on.

It's been nearly two years since Ben visited the city of Mathamagical. Now he must return to the lands beyond the skirting board though this time his journey will take him to Alphabet City, in the land of the Alphas, to help defeat the evil witch Manarag. With her pet, the Raid Pestgin, Manarag has come to this realm to jumble up all the words and remove all colour from language.

Join Ben as he journeys across Diction Land to find his friend and stop all language from suffering extinction.

"A fantastically clever way of teaching a child English" The Wishing Shelf Book Awards

RED RIBBON winner in The Wishing Shelf Book Awards

ISBN: 978-1291413144

Available on Amazon

A COMPLETE (at the time of going to press) COLLECTION OF POETRY

THE BOOK OF COLIN
C J DAVIES

Foreword by
Trevor Meaney

Tthe Book of Colin is a collection of poetry covering a wide array of subjects that range from the serious matters of hate and love, memories of childhood and the loss of a parent, to historical ghost stories and an affection for the number 5.

Colin has gathered together all his poetry works into one place as an attempt to provide the reader with an opportunity to glean some form of personal insight or deeper connection to the subject and the feelings of the writer.

Connecting with the author on a level that may not have been intended, but is certainly there, is one of the great joys of the written word. While poetry has primarily been a means of personal expression for Colin through the years, it is his hope that in taking the time to look through this collection, you find a piece that also means something to you.

And if he manages to do this, while at the same time making the name 'Colin' cool, he'll be a very happy man indeed.

ISBN: 978-1291748826

Available on Amazon

X-RAY SPECS

ONLY $1.00

An Hilarious Optical Illusion

Scientific optical principle really works. Imagine—you put on the "X-Ray" Specs and hold your hand in front of you. You seem to be able to look right through the flesh and see the bones underneath. Look at your friend. Is that really his body you "see" under his clothes? Loads of laughs and fun at parties. Send only $1 plus 25c shipping charges. Money Back Guarantee.
HONOR HOUSE PRODUCTS CORP., Lynbrook, N.Y. Dept. 97XR02

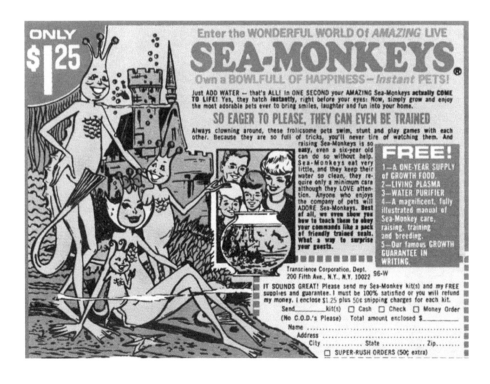

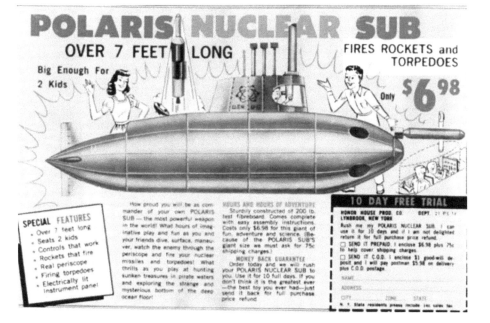